OXFORD
UNIVERSITY PRESS

Public Art

Chantelle Greenhills

Contents

Introduction 3

Public Places 6

A Colourful Toilet! 8

Sculptures of Presidents 10

Lights 12

Ice Carving 14

   The Ice Hotel 16

Trees and Bushes 18

Sand Sculpture 20

Graffiti 22

Index 24

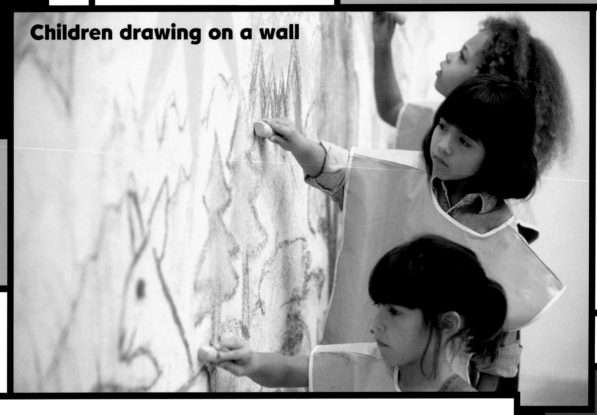

Children drawing on a wall

All around the world you can see public art. Public art is art that everyone can look at.

A painting on a wall is called a mural

Public art can be buildings. Public art can be murals. Public art can be sculptures.

Stone carvings on Easter Island

Public art can be made out of all sorts of things. Some public art is made using paint. Some public art is made using sand or ice. Some public art is made of recycled things.

Public Places

This statue is made out of bronze

Public places like parks and town squares often have public art in them. They may have statues or something that tells the history of them.

6

This fountain is in London

Some public places have a statue of someone famous. Public art could also be a garden or a fountain.

A Colourful Toilet!

Bottles are used in the windows

This toilet is a form of public art. It is in New Zealand. It was made by a famous artist.

The walls are different colours

The toilet is very bright. Glass bottles were used for some windows. It even has a living tree growing in it.

Sculptures of Presidents

Faces carved into rock

These sculptures are in the USA. The sculptures are carved into rock. They are 18 m high.

George Washington

The faces are of four presidents of the USA. They are George Washington, Thomas Jefferson, Theodore Roosevelt and Abraham Lincoln.

Shops are sometimes lit up

Lights can be a form of public art. Some buildings are lit up every night.

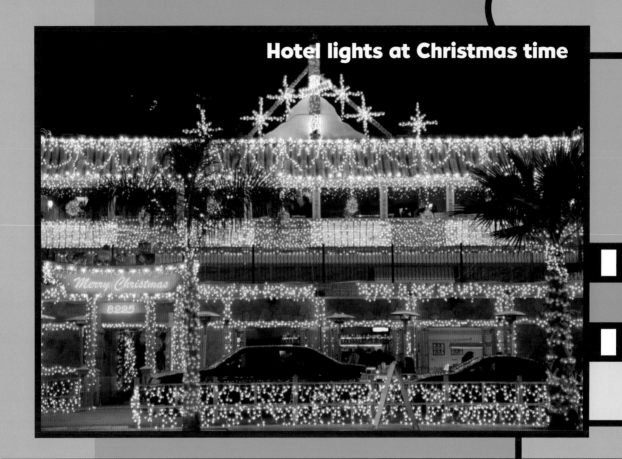

Hotel lights at Christmas time

Merry Christmas
8225

Sometimes houses and buildings are lit up for special occasions.

Ice Carving

Hard at work on an ice sculpture

Sometimes carvings are made out of blocks of ice. Special tools are used to make ice carvings.

This building is made of ice

Some ice carvings are small. They sit on tables at special occasions. Some ice carvings are big. You could walk into them.

The Ice Hotel

The Ice Hotel is in Quebec, Canada. The Ice Hotel is made of ice and snow. It is open from January until March. Then it starts to melt.

This is the dining room in the hotel

Most of the things at the Ice Hotel are made of ice or snow. The buildings and beds are made of ice. Even the plates are made of ice.

Trees and Bushes

A topiary garden

Trees can be cut into shapes to make public art. This is called topiary.

A gardener making a topiary bird

Some trees are made into ball shapes. Some trees are made into tower shapes. Some trees are made into animal shapes.

Sand Sculpture

A sand dragon

Some public art is made of sand. Very wet sand is used to make the sculptures. Water is the glue that holds the sculptures together.

A city made from sand

The sand can be made into towers. The sand can be made into walls. The sand can be made into arches. Special tools are used to carve the sand.

Graffiti

Graffiti on a wall

Sometimes people write and draw on walls and they are not allowed to. This is called graffiti. Some people think that graffiti is art. Some graffiti is painted with a paint can. Some graffiti is painted with a brush.

Chalk drawing on concrete is public art.

Public art is all around us. Have a look where you live. There is sure to be some to look at.

Index

building/s 4, 12, 13, 15, 17
fountain 7
garden 7, 18
houses 13
ice 5, 14, 15, 16, 17
mural/s 4
paint 5, 22
park/s 6
sand 5, 20, 21
statue 6, 7
tools 14, 21
tree/s 9, 18, 19
walls 9, 21, 22

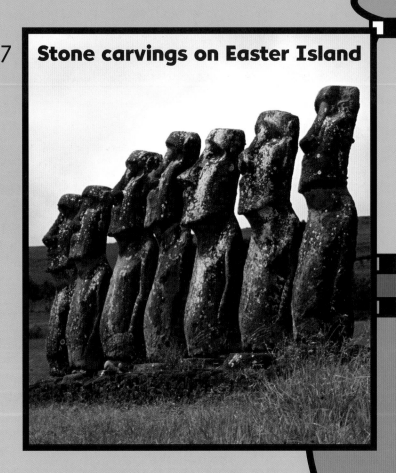

Stone carvings on Easter Island